ILLUMINATION PRESENTS
DESPICABLE ME3 ™

ANNUAL 2018

DESPICABLE ME 3: ANNUAL 2018

A CENTUM BOOK 9781911460664

PUBLISHED IN GREAT BRITAIN BY CENTUM BOOKS LTD

THIS EDITION PUBLISHED 2017

© 2017 UNIVERSAL STUDIOS.

1 3 5 7 9 10 8 6 4 2

CENTUM BOOKS LTD, 20 DEVON SQUARE, NEWTON ABBOT, DEVON, TQ12 2HR, UK

BOOKS@CENTUMBOOKSLTD.CO.UK

CENTUM BOOKS LIMITED REG. NO. 07641486

A CIP CATALOGUE RECORD FOR THIS BOOK IS AVAILABLE FROM THE BRITISH LIBRARY

PRINTED IN CHINA

CONTENTS

WELCOME, SPY!

Are you ready for all the fun inside this bumper-packed, action-packed, Minion-packed book?

You've come to the right place if you're looking for the lowdown on all your favourite gadgets from Despicable Me 3. Not forgetting tips on how to maximise your inner spy.

Villains beware, once you've read this book, you're going to be as **masterful as Gru!**

ARE YOU READY?
Then write your **super spy** name below:

DESPICABLE GALLERY

Welcome, spy fan! Read about your favourite **Despicable Me 3** heroes and villains in this gallery, then count all the Minions.

HOW MANY CAN YOU SPOT?

GRU:
Former super-villain turned super-spy. Creator of gadgets and father to Margo, Edith and Agnes.

LOVES: Gadgets and his family.

DISLIKES: Hugs. Don't get too close!

LUCY:
Secret agent, now full-time mum to Margo, Edith and Agnes. Eternal optimist and all round go-getter.

LOVES: Her girls and Kung fu.

DISLIKES: Anyone who might hurt her family.

MARGO:
Has a serious case of the teenage grumps, but is the best big sister to Edith and Agnes.

LOVES: Her sisters.

DISLIKES: Cheese and pigs.

8

ANSWERS ON PAGE 75

EDITH:
Loves to play jokes, devise pranks and cause a bit of mischief wherever she goes. She's always planning her next stunt.

LOVES: Devising pranks and playing pranks!

DISLIKES: Having nothing to do.

AGNES:
The littlest member of Gru's crew is also the sweetest. Most importantly, she loves unicorns.

LOVES: Unicorns of course!

DISLIKES: Agnes doesn't really dislike anything.

DRU:
Who knew Gru had a twin? He lives on Freedonia; famous for pig farming and cheese!

LOVES: Fast cars and his palatial mansion.

DISLIKES: Not being able to live out his super-villain dream.

CLIVE THE ROBOT:
Absolutely the best sidekick any 80s-loving super-villain could ever wish for!

LOVES: Playing 80s tracks.

DISLIKES: Being a robot.

BALTHAZAR BRATT:
Child prodigy and criminal mastermind, this 80s-loving super villain is ready for world domination..

LOVES: The 80s, jazzercise and his Keytar.

DISLIKES: Hollywood because they cancelled his TV show, 'Evil Bratt'.

WE ARE FAMILY!

Colour in Gru's family portrait and **decorate the frame with your doodles.**

Who else can you spot **HANGING OUT?**

Can you spot the members of Gru's family in the tree?

○ GRU   ○ MARGO

○ LUCY   ○ EDITH

○ AGNES   ○ DRU

ANSWERS ON PAGE 75

YOUR FAMILY TREE

Make your own family tree! **Doodle your family members in the frames and write their names underneath.**

BALTHAZAR BRATT

Introducing a new super-villain! This 80s-loving, shoulder-pad wearing, jazzercise dancer is a criminal mastermind. He's an evil genius who may just be Gru's toughest challenge yet.

Read these Balthazar Bratt fact blasts!

80s MULLET

FASHIONABLE
POLO NECK
(IN THE 80s)

EXTREME
SHOULDER-PADS

GROOVY
KEYTAR

SNAZZY WHITE
DANCING SHOES

FAVOURITE TUNE:
Anything involving synths.

VILLAIN LAIR:
An ocean-based homage to the 80s, complete with colourful tower and security bots galore!

FAVOURITE GADGET:
Keeping the 80s dream alive with his Keytar!

DRESS SENSE:
Purple, shiny and tight.

SECRET WEAPON:
This super-villain is very good at disguises.

EVIL SIDEKICK:
Clive the Robot.

FAMOUS FOR:
Being an 80s child TV star in his show EVIL BRATT.

DANCE PARTY!

Check out these dance poses of Bratt's.

Select your favourite poses, then create a dance sequence by writing the pose order on the line below, then get your groove on Bratt style.

1   2   3   4   5   6

_____

SPOT THE BOT!

CAN YOU SPOT FIVE DIFFERENCES BETWEEN THESE TWO PICTURES OF CLIVE?

1   2

ANSWERS ON
page 75

13

BUBBLE TROUBLE

Bratt was after the most expensive gem in the world:
THE DUMONT DIAMOND.

Dressed in scuba gear and performing a moonwalking dance manoeuvre across the ocean, Bratt sneaked on board the transport ship that was transporting the diamond.

He removed bubblegum from his mouth and threw it near an approaching guard. The guard didn't think anything of it, until the gum started to expand, covering him and the entire deck in bright pink bubbles.

Underneath the ocean waves, using AVL mini-subs, Agents "Grucy" (Gru and Lucy's nickname!) and Minions, Dave and Jerry, were on their way to the transport ship.

At the push of a button, Gru transformed their mini-subs into jet bikes, and they raced towards the ship.

"TOO LATE AGAIN, GRU," Bratt taunted from the ship, which was now covered in bubblegum bubbles and rising into the air. Bratt was escaping with the diamond! The agents had missed the boat.

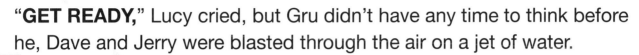

"**GET READY,**" Lucy cried, but Gru didn't have any time to think before he, Dave and Jerry were blasted through the air on a jet of water.

"Go get him, Gru-Gru!" said Lucy lovingly, as Gru landed with a thump on the deck of the pink-bubblegum coated ship.

"How's your transition coming?" said Bratt, standing before Gru. "You know, from world's worst villain to world's worst agent?"

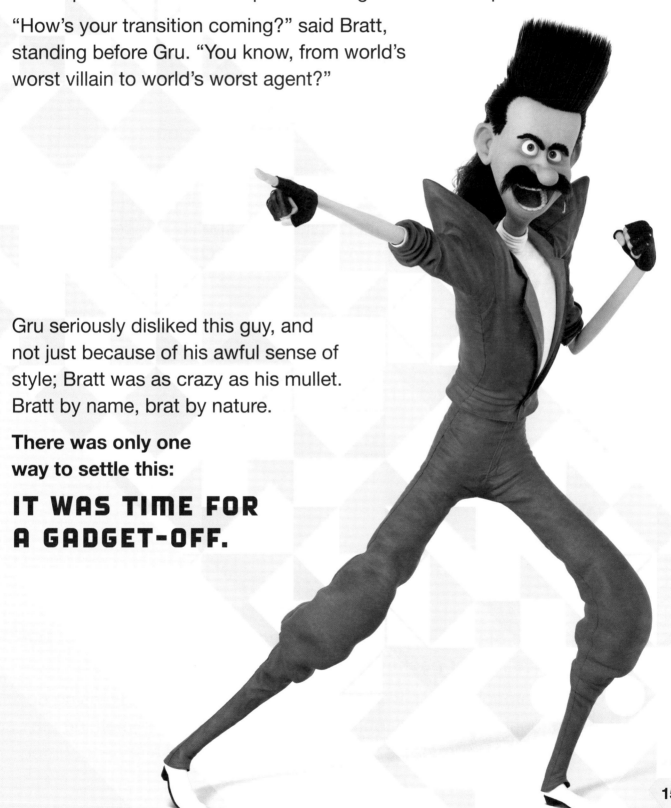

Gru seriously disliked this guy, and not just because of his awful sense of style; Bratt was as crazy as his mullet. Bratt by name, brat by nature.

There was only one way to settle this:

IT WAS TIME FOR A GADGET-OFF.

BUBBLE TROUBLE

But then 80s-loving Bratt had a better, groovier idea.

To settle matters once and for all, he proposed a dance-off.

Gru watched with disgust as Bratt danced. Gru waited patiently for Bratt to finish his routine and then pulled off a special dance move of his own, knocking out Bratt and then grabbing the diamond.

BUT IT WASN'T OVER YET.

A sonic wave blasted Gru across the deck and over the side of the ship – Bratt's Keytar packed some serious synth.

As Gru fell through the air, it looked as though the ocean was rising up to meet him, until suddenly he found himself caught up in something pink and sticky. The bubblegum had saved him from a deadly watery encounter!

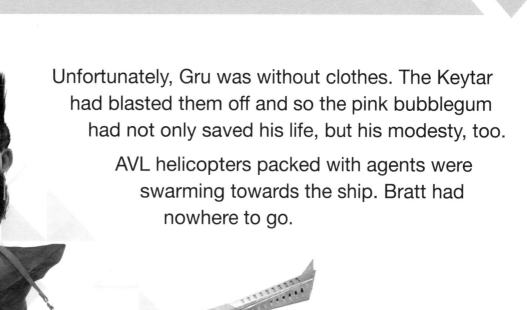

Unfortunately, Gru was without clothes. The Keytar had blasted them off and so the pink bubblegum had not only saved his life, but his modesty, too.

AVL helicopters packed with agents were swarming towards the ship. Bratt had nowhere to go.

"SON OF A BETAMAX!"

cried Bratt in frustration. Running towards the edge of the ship, Bratt threw himself into the air and deployed a wing suit.

"THIS IS NOT OVER, GRU!"

Bratt shouted as he escaped. Gru may not have caught Bratt, but at least he had the diamond.

If you're wondering what happened to Dave and Jerry, they landed safely on an island and watched everything unfold from a DJ booth at a beach party.

NAUGHTY MINIONS!

Oh dear, after saying goodbye to Gru, things really go bad for the Minions and they wind up in jail.

Help the Minions escape and get back to their master Gru by finding a path through this jail maze!

START

FINISH

ANSWERS ON PAGE 75

BAD COLOURING

Try the funny colouring challenges and colour in these naughty Minions.
How bad will your colouring be?

Colour in this Minion using a different hand than you usually use to write.

Colour in this Minion using your toes instead of your fingers.

Colour in this Minion without looking at the page.

TRUE UNICORN

Agnes loves unicorns, sooooooo much!

Only one of the pictures below matches the big unicorn picture. Can you spot it?

Where does Agnes venture on her hunt for a unicorn?

ANSWERS ON PAGE 75

UNICORN YOURSELF!

Make your own unicorn horn that you can wear to a party, or every day if you wish. **You can be a unicorn (or uni-goat!) to your heart's content!**

ASK A GROWN-UP TO HELP YOU WHEN CRAFTING

YOU WILL NEED:

* Unicorn horn template
* Glue or tape
* Two pieces of ribbon approx. 30 cm
* Decorations such as glitter glue, sequins, sparkly paint or ribbon

1

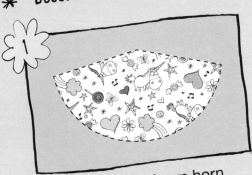

Press out the unicorn horn template from your card press-outs.

2

Colour in or paint the template or use glue to stick on decorations.

3

Roll the press-out into the unicorn horn shape and fix the sides together using glue or tape.

4

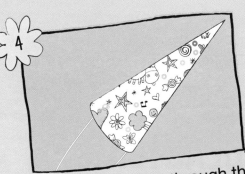

Thread the ribbon through the holes and tie in place with a knot. Place the horn on your head, then tie the two pieces of ribbon together under your chin.

GADGETS GALORE!

Don't you just love a good gadget? Gadgets can get you out of tight situations when faced with a super-villain or super-spy.

Read about some of the gadgets and vehicles in Despicable Me 3. Which is your favourite?

MINI-SUBS

If you need to zoom underwater at high speed, then these are just the ticket.

JET BIKES

For all your above-water needs, Jet Bikes will get you from A to super-villain in no time.

FART BLASTER

Perfect for when you need to clear a room. Just make sure you have a gas mask.

Can you spot the Minions' favourite gadget on these pages?

?

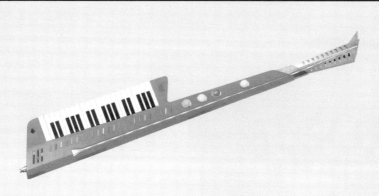

KEYTAR

Are you a fan of the 80s AND a super-villain? Then a Keytar complete with sonic blaster is likely right up your street.

GRAPPLE GUN

This gadget is perfect for scaling tall buildings or super-villain lairs.

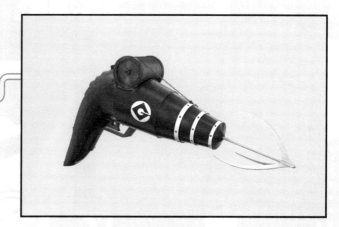

DRU'S CAR

This is not just any car, my friends! It's a sports car crossed with a spaceship and does just about anything, including 0 to 400 in 3 seconds! In Gru's words, "Holey, moley!"

GOODBYE, GRU!

It was a bad day for Gru when he lost his job and then all the Minions. **(Well, apart from Dave and Jerry!)**

Colour in the Minions as they say goodbye to Gru.

Maybe blue would be an appropriate colour for this sad occasion!

MINIONS AND THEIR MASTER

I'VE BEEN A
BAD BOY

REVENGE ON HOLLYWOOD
CHECKLIST

Being the world's most wanted super-villain takes a tiny bit of organisation.

Fill in the blanks using the words below to complete Bratt's checklist.

DIAMOND	ACTION FIGURE	JAZZERCISE
CLIVE	OCEAN	HOLLYWOOD

1   **Build** an impenetrable and totally groovy lair in the middle of the _____ .

2   **Ask** _____ to compile my ultimate 80s mix-tape.

3   **Steal** the Dumont _____ .

4   **Finish** building the giant _____ _____ of EVIL BRATT.

5   _____ myself to my ultimate **amazing self**.

6   Use diamond to **seek revenge** on _____ and the world!

ANSWERS ON
page 75

WHO SAID WHAT?

Read these quotes and work out who said what by **matching the words to the pictures!**

 1 "HOLEY, MOLEY!"

 2 "I NEED TO GET TO BED SO I CAN WAKE UP AND FIND A UNICORN. GOODNIGHT!"

 3 "LA PIZZA!"

 4 "BAM! I AM A GREAT MOTHER!"

ANSWERS ON PAGE 75

THE UNICORN QUEST

Help Agnes and Edith track down the unicorn in the Crooked Forest by following the directions. **Start your quest in square A10.**

TIP: Once you have found the spot, Lay out some candy and wait.

MOVE:

1. 3 Squares East

2. 5 Squares North

3. 2 Squares West

4. 3 Squares North:

5. 7 Squares East

6. 3 Squares South

	A	B	C	D	E	F	G	H	I	J
1										
2										
3										
4										
5										
6										
7										
8										
9										
10	START									

DID YOU KNOW?

The man in the town tells Agnes something important about her quest:

"If a maiden pure of heart goes into the Crooked Forest, the unicorn will come and be hers forever."

ANSWERS ON PAGE 75

MISSING THEIR BIG BOSS!

It doesn't take long for Mel to realise how much he misses his boss and to begin planning the Minions' prison escape. **Search this Minion-packed scene and find all the map-holding Minions.** There are 20 to find!

ANSWERS ON PAGE 75

THE CAR CHASE

Dru had just revealed his big secret. Well, their father's big secret. Underneath Dru's Freedonian mansion was their father's super-villain lair. The pigs and cheese were just a front for their father's super-villain empire.

Dru wanted Gru to teach him everything about being a super-villain because their father never had, but Gru refused – he had put that life behind him.

Although Gru was tempted, after all it was the MOST awesome lair that he had ever seen, packed with high-tech computers, holograms and gadgets.

Dru innocently pulled a lever and the floor opened, revealing an AMAZING-looking villain vehicle. It looked like a sports car crossed with a spaceship!

"Holey-moley!" cried Gru. He was in love.

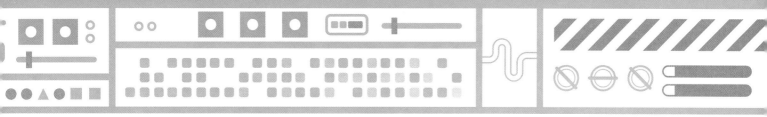

"Dad's villain wheels. Pretty slick, huh?" said Dru, lying across the car. "Want to take her out for a spin? Just for fun?"

Gru didn't need to be asked twice. Soon they were speeding through the Freedonian countryside. Dru wasn't the best driver though, he knocked over fences and narrowly missed some pedestrians.

Dru explained the car's super villain worthy features. The vehicle did 0 to 400 in 3 seconds, was able to withstand a nuclear blast and was filled to the brim with gadgets. Gru was impressed.

After dodging a tractor, Dru accidentally sped off a cliff, but he wasn't worried at all.

WITH THE PRESS OF A BUTTON, GRAPPLING HOOKS PULLED THE CAR TO SAFETY.

THE CAR CHASE

As they headed into a village, Dru wanted to impress Gru even more by showing him how villainous he could be. "**Wait for me here!**" he told Gru as he disappeared into a sweet truck.

A minute later Dru was back having stolen some lollipops. Dru thought it was a big deal. Gru was trying to look impressed when they both heard a familiar noise!

It was the Freedonian police and they were chasing them on bicycles.

Now in the driver's seat, Gru accelerated away. He realised that he was actually enjoying himself.

When they met some pigs blocking the road, Gru instinctively pressed a button and the car shot up on stilts. The police officers weren't so lucky, as they ended up riding on the backs of the pigs after crashing into them head first.

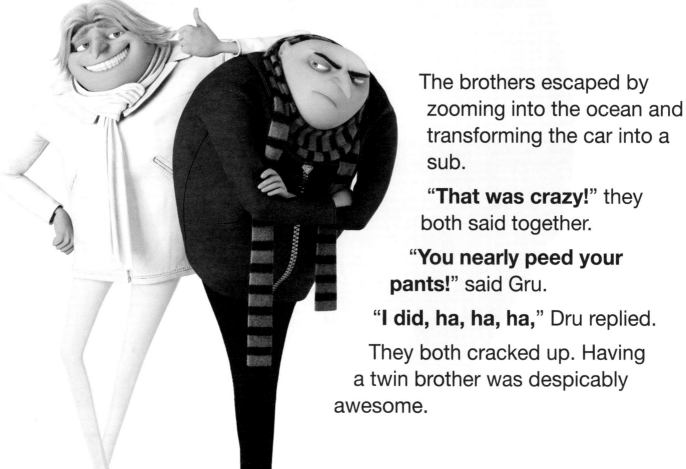

The brothers escaped by zooming into the ocean and transforming the car into a sub.

"That was crazy!" they both said together.

"You nearly peed your pants!" said Gru.

"I did, ha, ha, ha," Dru replied.

They both cracked up. Having a twin brother was despicably awesome.

35

FUN IN FREEDONIA!

Freedonia is famous for its pigs and its cheese.

Dru's family are excited about staying there and discovering more about their new home.

Imagine if you had your own country, what would you call it?

Name your country:

_____

What three things would your country be famous for?

1

2

3

Invent three rules that everyone should live by:

1

2

3

Design your own flag:

When Gru's family arrive in Freedonia by Dru's private jet, they love it!

CHEESY SEQUENCES

When Lucy and the girls go to the Freedonian Cheese Festival they discover how much the Freedonian people really love cheese; there are even cheese hats and jewellery!

Can you solve these cheesy sequences?

WHICH PIECE OF CHEESE FITS?

A   B   C

ANSWERS ON PAGE 76

LAUGH WITH EDITH

As we know, Edith loves playing a prank or two, but she also loves jokes. **Here are some of her favourite jokes inspired by her time in Freedonia!**

Q: WHAT DO YOU CALL CHEESE THAT IS SAD?
A: BLUE CHEESE.

Q: WHAT DO PIGS GET WHEN THEY'RE ILL?
A: OINKMENT!

Q: HOW DO PIGS WRITE TOP-SECRET MESSAGES?
A: WITH INVISIBLE OINK!

Q: WHY DID THE PIG CROSS THE ROAD?
A: HE GOT BOARED.

Q: WHAT DO YOU CALL A PIG THIEF?
A: A HAMBURGLAR.

Q: WHAT CHEESE DO BEAVERS LIKE?
A: EDAM

Q: WHEN SHOULD YOU KEEP AN EYE ON YOUR CHEESE?
A: WHEN IT'S UP TO NO GOUDA.

CREATE A ROBOT SIDEKICK

Invent your own robot sidekick.

Doodle and write about it below.

Draw it HERE:

Make a face!

Add buttons and lights.

Add some fun graphics to give your robot a personality.

WRITE ABOUT YOUR NEW SIDEKICK!

My robot's name is: _____

It loves to: _____

Its secret power is: _____

RACE TO THE DIAMOND

On board the ship, Gru needs to find Bratt and the diamond before he can escape. **Help Gru through the maze to Bratt.**

FINISH

START

GRU VS DRU

When Gru meets his twin brother Dru, he couldn't be more excited. But his excitement doesn't last for long when he discovers that they are very different from one another.

Which statement belongs to which brother?

1 Doesn't like his personal space invaded. No hugs please!

2 This guy is the life and soul of the party.

3 Instantly likeable and loveable with a winning smile.

4 A gadget mastermind and super-spy genius.

5 A wannabe super-villain – he has all the gear but no idea.

6 This guy has put his super-villain days behind him.

42

ANSWERS ON PAGE 76

SPY VS VILLAIN

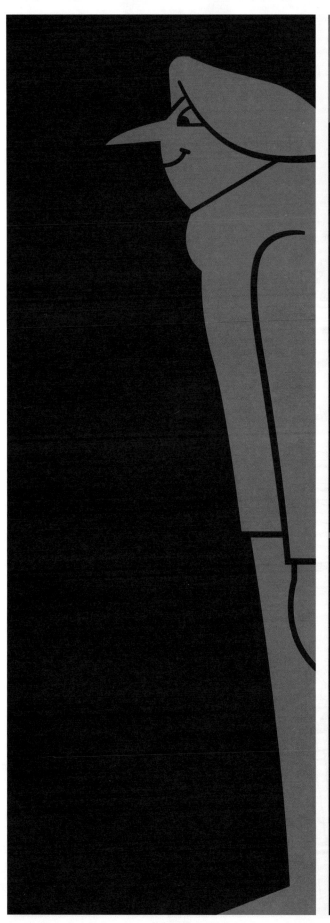

ONE BIG, HAPPY FAMILY

SPY VS VILLAIN

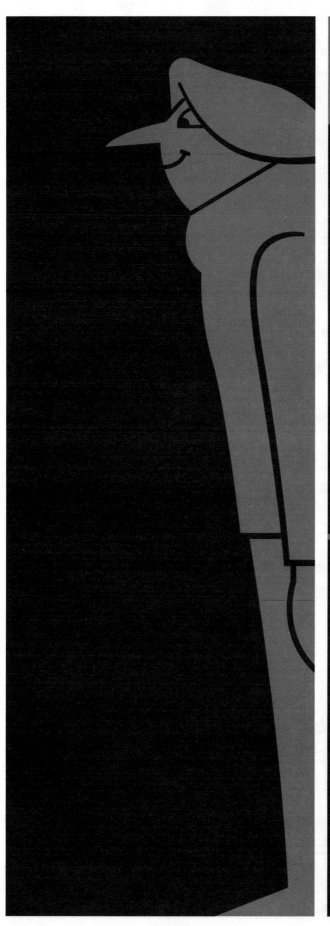

ONE BiG, HAPPY FAMiLY

RAINBOW MATCHING

Agnes thinks that rainbows are so AMAZING!
Can you find all the matching pairs of rainbows?

Which rainbow is the odd one out?

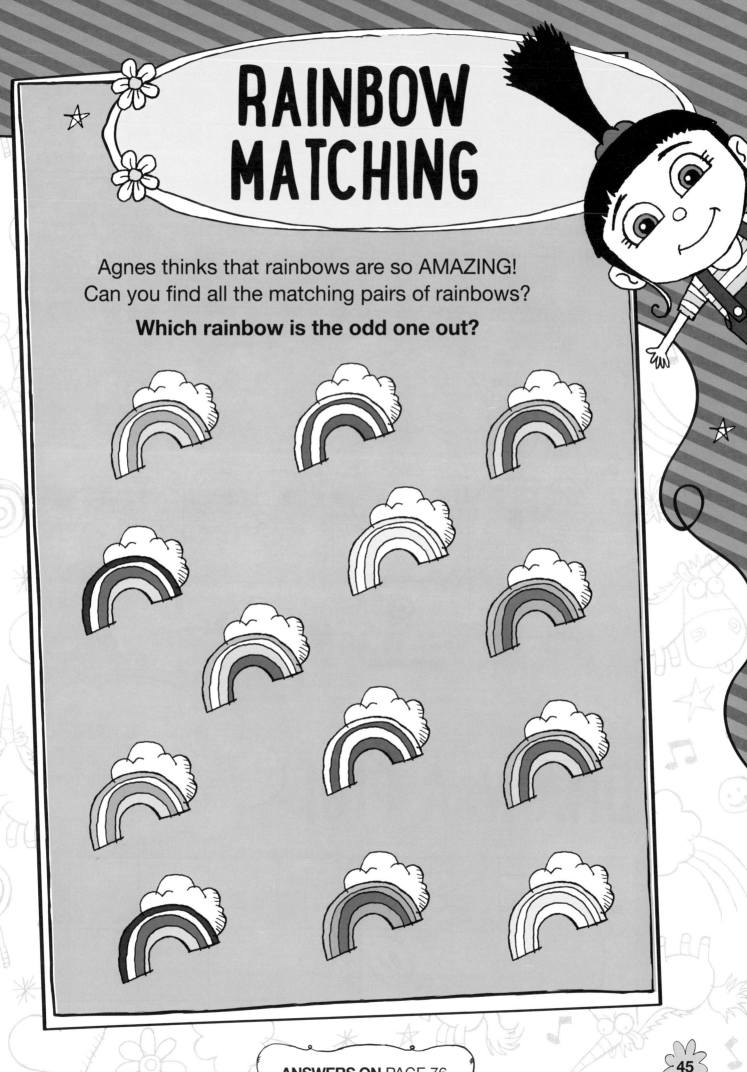

ANSWERS ON PAGE 76

SELFIE DOT-TO-DOT

Complete this dot-to-dot of the Minions taking a selfie with the pigs in Freedonia. The pigs seem to really like the Minions – or is it the other way around?

DRAW A PIG!

Draw and colour your own pig in the box below using the grid to help you.

TIKI TIME

Help Dave and Jerry get to the **tiki party** in time!

FINISH

START

ANSWERS ON PAGE 76

47

ASSEMBLE THE MINIONS!

All your favourite Minions are waiting to be assembled! Follow the step-by-step instructions and soon enough you'll have your own loyal army of Minions! (If you need help, don't be afraid to ask a grown-up.)

DIRECTIONS
BASIC MINION ASSEMBLY

1. Carefully press out each piece along the perforated lines.
2. Bend the scored lines.
3. Form the main body shape into a rectangular cube and insert the main body tab into the opposite slit. (Figure 1)
4. Hold the cube so that the bottom of the Minion is visible and insert all three tabs into the slits at the same time. (Figure 2)
5. Repeat step 4 for the top of the Minion.

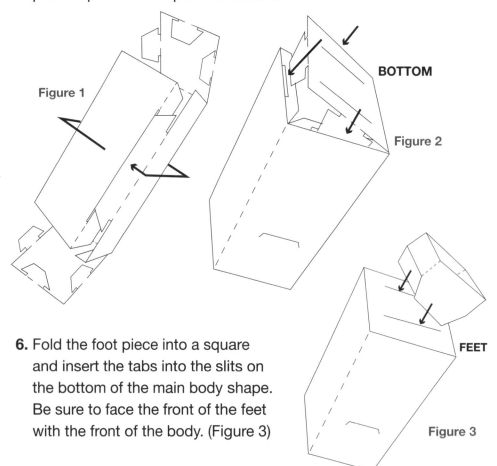

Figure 1

BOTTOM

Figure 2

FEET

6. Fold the foot piece into a square and insert the tabs into the slits on the bottom of the main body shape. Be sure to face the front of the feet with the front of the body. (Figure 3)

Figure 3

7. With the Minion body upright, squeeze at the folds near the upper side slits to allow space and insert the goggle tab. Repeat on the other side. (Figure 4)

Figure 4

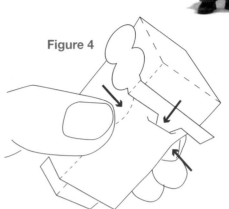

8. Many of these Minions have hair. Insert the tabs into the top of the head. Use a pencil or rod to curl the two halves, then insert both middle tabs into the central slit on the top of the head. Insert each single tab into its own slit. (Figure 5)

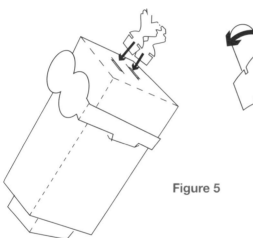

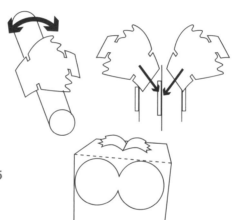

Figure 5

9. Insert the arm tabs into the side slits. If the arm is double-sided, fold it over before inserting both tabs into the same slit. (Figure 6)

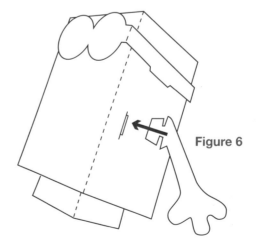

Figure 6

NOTE: The codes on the tabs for the arms, eyes, feet, hats, and hair correspond to the location on the main body:

MA = Minion Arm
MB = Minion Body
MF = Minion Foot
MB = Minion Body
MG = Minion Googles
MM = Minion Manacle

For example, tab A1 (the arm) goes into slit A1 on the main body.

THE CROOKED FOREST

When the family went to visit Gru's new-found twin brother, Dru, in Freedonia, Agnes heard about a local legend.

The legend stated that **REAL UNICORNS** roamed the nearby forest.

At the Freedonian Cheese Festival, Edith and Agnes met a man who told them all about the legend.

Edith thought it was all a fake.
"It's real all right!" the one-eyed man told them, **"I saw one once with my own eye."**

Agnes couldn't wait to hear more!

"What did it look like? Did you pet it? Did it smell like candy? Was it fluffy?" she asked excitedly.

"It was so fluffy," the one-eyed man told her.

"Do you think I could find one, too?" Agnes wondered.

"They say if a maiden pure of heart goes into the Crooked Forest the unicorn will come and be hers forever."

Agnes and Edith set off into the forest, determined to find a MYSTICAL UNICORN.

THE CROOKED FOREST

It would fulfil Agnes' lifelong dream to find and become friends with a unicorn, and Edith's more recent dream of (in case unicorns did exist) filming a unicorn and selling the video to become rich.

They walked for a long time in the forest until they came to a beautiful clearing.

"THIS IS IT! THIS IS WHERE WE ARE GOING TO FIND THE UNICORN!" Agnes declared.

Agnes emptied out her pockets and bag, piling up candy, liquorice and marshmallows. It was unicorn bait; now all they had to do was wait.

"CAN WE GO BACK NOW?" asked Edith after a while. Well, a **LONG** while.

"ALREADY?! IT'S ONLY BEEN EIGHT HOURS," Agnes replied.

Edith thought they should go before it got dark, but Agnes wanted to wait a bit longer.

Suddenly there was a sound. "My whole life has been building up to this moment!" whispered Agnes.

A little white goat with one horn broken off appeared. Edith knew it was a goat, but Agnes thought it was a UNICORN!

"I'M GOING TO NAME YOU LUCKY," said Agnes. Lucky licked Agnes' face. Agnes was in unicorn heaven. Her dream had finally come true!

Edith didn't want to burst Agnes' bubble, so it was up to Gru to explain to Agnes that Lucky wasn't really a unicorn.

But it turned out it didn't matter at all, because Agnes loved Lucky, whether he was a unicorn or not.

MY ULTIMATE LAIR

Gru discovers that his brother Dru really wants to be a super-villain (just like their dad!) and that under Dru's Freedonian mansion lies the most amazing villain lair EVER. **Design your own lair below.**

List five Gru-worthy features about your lair:

1
2
3
4
5

MATCH THE GADGETS

Dru has a lot to learn about super-villainy.

Can you help Dru work out which shadow belongs to which gadget?

 1

 A

2

B

3

C

4

D

5

E

ANSWERS ON PAGE 76

SPY THE DIFFERENCE

Test your spy skills and spot the differences between the pictures on these pages. There are three challenges – easy, medium and hard. **Can you spy them all?**

1 LEVEL **EASY**

Using your best spy skills, can you spot **five differences** between the two Minion pictures below?

2 LEVEL **MEDIUM**

Now, can you spot **seven differences** between the two Agents "Grucy" pictures below?

56

ANSWERS ON PAGE 76

③  **LEVEL HARD**

Finally, can you spot **ten differences** between these two Gru and Dru pictures?

RAINBOW COOKIES

Make these yummy Agnes-approved rainbow cookies.
Perfect to share with friends or pet unicorns!

INGREDIENTS:
* 140g icing sugar
* 1 tsp vanilla extract
* 1 egg yolk
* 250g butter
* 375g flour
* Rainbow sprinkles

YOU'LL ALSO NEED:
* A mixing bowl
* Wooden spoon
* Lined baking tray
* Cooling rack
* Cookie cutter

TiP
You can also add more sprinkles to the top of your cookies to make them extra colourful!

1 Ask an adult to preheat the oven to 190°C.

2 Use a wooden spoon to mix together the butter, icing sugar, vanilla and the egg yolk in the bowl. Mix until they form a creamy texture.

3 Now add the sprinkles! Mix until the sprinkles are evenly distributed.

4 Add in the flour a little bit at a time until it forms a dough.

5 Wrap the dough in cling film and chill it in the fridge for around 30 mins.

6 Spread some flour on the work surface and roll out the dough with a rolling pin. Use a cookie cutter to cut out shapes, then carefully put them on a lined baking tray.

7 Ask an adult to put the tray into the oven and bake for about 10-12 minutes until they are lightly golden brown.

8 Ask an adult to remove the cookies from the oven and to carefully slide them off the tray on to a cooling rack. Leave to cool and then enjoy!

LUCKY COLOURING

Colour in this sweet picture of Agnes with Lucky!

Decorate the page with rainbow confetti and magical doodles!

BAD STRIPES

Give these Minions a jail makeover using a black pen.
Doodle stripes on their overalls. Of course, if you're forgiving you could add different patterns!

NAUGHTY MINIONS!

WHO SAID WHAT?

Read these quotes and work out who said what by **matching the words to the pictures!**

1. "I'VE BEEN A BAD BOY."

2. "I'VE LEFT THAT LIFE BEHIND ME. END OF STORY."

3. "DAD'S LAIR! TA-DA!"

4. "GO GET HIM, GRU-GRU!"

A

B

C

D

ANSWERS ON PAGE 76

I ♥ THE 80S!

Balthazar Bratt, former 80s TV child star, lover of shoulder pads and big hair, is as dastardly at heart as his outfits. He's EVIL! **Colour him in, 80s style.**

BALTHAZAR'S COLOURING TIPS:

IT'LL BE A FASHION SMASH HIT IF YOU USE COLOURS THAT **CLASH.**

MAKE THE WORLD BRIGHTER AND USE **NEON.**

I LOVE BABY BLUES AND POWDER PINKS.

DREAM UP A **GHASTLY NEW HAIRSTYLE** FOR BALTHAZAR IN THIS BOX.

MINION MAKEOVER

Now give the Minions an 80s makeover with your colouring pens.

Doodle on some Bratt-worthy mullets and banana-shaped keytars.

RATE YOUR MAKEOVERS FROM BEST TO WORST.

WRITE EITHER 1ST, 2ND OR 3RD IN THE BOXES NEXT TO EACH MINION.

TIKI PARTY TIME

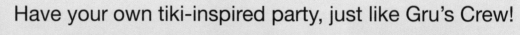

Have your own tiki-inspired party, just like Gru's Crew!

Use the press-outs to create decorations, then organise your party.

MAKE TIKI BUNTING

You will need:

* Tiki press-outs
* One long piece of string
* Short pieces of ribbon
* Tape or sticky tack
* Colouring pencils and pens

ALWAYS ask permission before hanging decorations and ask for a grown-up's help when using scissors.

TIP
Bunting can look great above a doorway!

Take each press-out and colour it in.

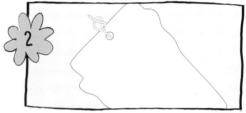

Thread the short pieces of ribbon and thread through the holes in each press-out. Do this for each press-out.

Next tie each press-out on to the long piece of string using the ribbon. TIP: Tie the ribbon tightly so the decorations stay in place.

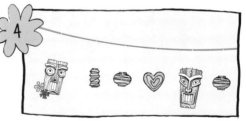

Now ask an adult to help you hang up your Tiki bunting, using tape or by tying the string up.

Now it's time to organise your AWESOME party using these Lists.

GUEST LIST:

1
2
3
4
5

FOOD:

1
2
3
4
5

Parties are so much fun, especially with your family!

GAMES:

1
2
3
4
5

MUSIC:

1
2
3
4
5

Gru and Dru approached Bratt's island fortress. It was covered in jagged, razor-sharp spikes.

"**TAKE THE WHEEL, DRU,**" ordered Gru as their boat got nearer.

Gru was about to break in and get the Dumont Diamond back from Balthazar Bratt's clutches.

Gru catapulted himself through the air and landed with an elegant slap against the fortress's enormous tower. He was about to start the ascent to the top when there was a loud

THUMP!

"Dru!" cried Gru. Dru was supposed to stay with the boat! But he didn't have time to be annoyed, as there was a security bot heading their way.

"**Camouflage mode now!**" Gru said urgently, pressing a button on his suit.

Luckily the robot didn't sense them, even though Dru nearly landed them in trouble as he fumbled with his suit controls.

"WE GOT IN!" Dru cried excitedly. But Gru wasn't as happy – in fact, he was super annoyed.

"THIS WAY!" ordered Gru. They emerged from a vent and found themselves inside Bratt's bedroom.

Bratt was asleep and snoozing like a baby, wearing the diamond. Stealthily Gru attempted to remove the diamond, but then Dru stepped on a noisy toy, setting off the intruder alarm! Gru and Dru rolled under the bed just in time. A startled Bratt got up and took the diamond with him.

Gru and Dru found themselves walking down a dark hallway full of glowing red lights.

The lights were actually the eyes from hundreds and hundreds of Bratt action figures. "Oh man!" cried Dru, picking one up. "These have the Mega Diamond Laser! These were so hard to find when I was a boy."

Gru hastily placed the doll back on the shelf and they continued down the hall, before entering Bratt's lab.

Dru was distracted once more by a giant vat of bubblegum. He sneaked a piece.

"FOCUS!" GRU TOLD HIM.

"Look at it, Clive, it's beautiful!"
It was Bratt. He was admiring a 100-foot tall Giant Bratt Action Figure. There was a ladder all the way from the floor to the top.

Unfortunately the gum Dru had stolen had started to expand in Dru's mouth and he could not contain it. Gru tried to help a spluttering Dru.

"INTRUDERS!" shouted Clive. They'd been spotted!

"There's two of you now?" asked a confused Bratt.
"Well, there's about to be none of you."

Gru performed the Heimlich manoeuvre on Dru – and the gum went flying, trapping Bratt and Clive in a sticky mess.

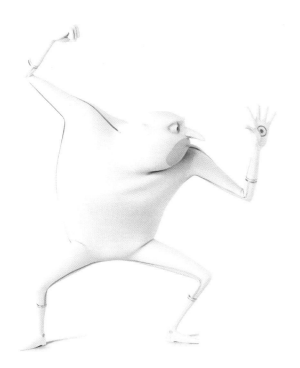

Gru grabbed the diamond and they both escaped the lab, but the action figures from earlier had been activated and were now chasing after Gru and Dru, firing lasers and missiles at them.

"Oh no!" said Gru as they neared the edge of the fortress roof.

"Oh no? What does that mean? **ARE WE GONNA DIE?**" asked Dru.

They were cornered with nowhere to go! Suddenly Dru's red helicopter appeared – it was Lucy! She was there to save the day.

They escaped with the diamond once more, dodging missiles as they went. **Bratt's plan was ruined. OR WAS IT?**

THE MOST DESPICABLE QUIZ EVER!

Test your spy knowledge in this ultimate Despicable Me 3 quiz.

1

Gru and Lucy get fired from where?

a) The Anti Spy League   b) The Anti Villain League

c) The Spy Villain League

2

What do the girls do for Gru and Lucy on their anniversary?

a) Throw them a surprise party!   b) Send them on holiday to Hawaii

c) Do a little dance

3

What is the name of the diamond that Bratt wants to steal?

a) The David Diamond   b) The Daisy Diamond   c) The Dumont Diamond

4

What sweet does Balthazar Bratt use to disable the transport ship?

a) Chocolate buttons   b) Mints   c) Bubblegum

5 What's the name of Balthazar Bratt's robot sidekick?
a) Clarissa   b) Clement   c) Clive

6 Who is the leader of the Minion rebellion?
a) Mel   b) Stuart   c) Tony

7 What's the name of the island where Gru's twin brother lives?
a) Treedonia   b) Freedonia   c) Cheesedonia

8 What does Gru find out about his brother Dru?
a) That he wants Gru to become a pig farmer
b) That he wants to be a super-villain   c) That he wants to be a super-spy

9 What did Balthazar Bratt used to be in the 80s?
a) A dance champion   b) A TV star   c) A super-spy

10 What do Gru and Dru discover at Bratt's fortress?
a) A giant teddy bear   b) A giant Bratt action figure   c) A giant rocket

ANSWERS ON PAGE 74

DESPICABLE QUIZ

▾ ANSWERS

1 Gru and Lucy get fired from **The Anti Villain League.**

2 The girls throw them **a surprise party!**

3 Bratt wants to steal **The Dumont Diamond.**

4 Bratt uses **bubblegum** to disable the transport ship.

5 Balthazar Bratt's robot sidekick is called **Clive.**

6 Mel is the leader of the **Minion rebellion.**

7 The island where Dru lives is called **Freedonia.**

8 Gru finds out that his brother wants to be **a super-villain.**

9 Balthazar Bratt used to be a **TV star.**

10 Gru and Dru discover a **giant Bratt action figure** at Bratt's fortress.

ANSWERS

PAGES 8-9
There are 8 Minions.

PAGE 10

PAGE 13

PAGE 18

PAGE 20

PAGE 27

1. Build an impenetrable and totally groovy lair in the middle of the **OCEAN.**
2. Ask **CLIVE** to compile my ultimate 80s mix-tape.
3. Steal the Dumont **DIAMOND.**
4. Finish building the giant **ACTION FIGURE** of EVIL BRATT.
5. **JAZZERCISE** myself to my ultimate amazing self.
6. Use diamond to seek revenge on **HOLLYWOOD** and the world!

PAGE 28
1-C, Gru (as Dru); **2-D**, Agnes;
3-B, Mel; **4-A**, Lucy.

PAGE 29

	A	B	C	D	E	F	G	H	I	J
1										
2										
3										
4										
5										
6										
7										
8										
9										
10	START									

PAGES 30-31

ANSWERS

PAGE 38

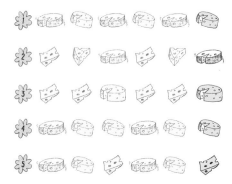

PAGE 41

PAGE 42

1 - Gru, 2 - Dru, 3 - Dru,
4 - Gru, 5 - Dru, 6 - Gru.

PAGE 45

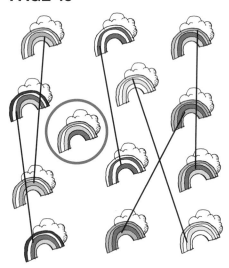

PAGE 47

PAGE 55

1 - C, 2 - D, 3 - E, 4 - A, 5 - B.

PAGES 56–57

1. Level **Easy**

2. Level **Medium**

3. Level **Hard**

PAGE 63

1 - **D** Balthazar Bratt, 2 - **A** Gru
3 - **B** Dru, 4 - **C** Lucy.

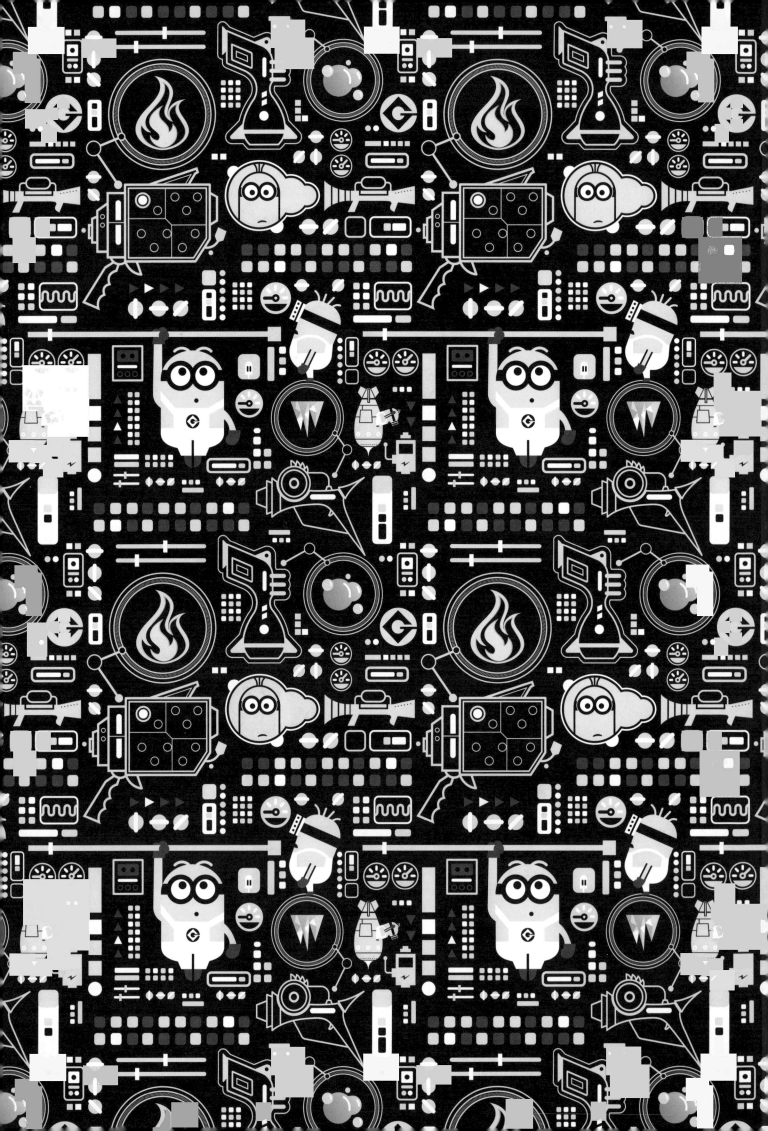